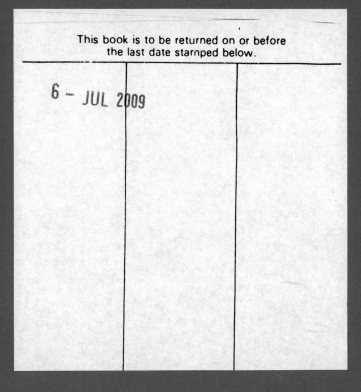

The European Union *Today*

The European Union *Today*

Simon Ponsford

FRANKLIN WATTS
LONDON • SYDNEY

Designer Peter Bailey/Proof Books
Editor Constance Novis
Art Director Jonathan Hair
Editor-in-Chief John C. Miles
Picture research Sarah Smithies

First published in 2007 by Franklin Watts

Franklin Watts
338 Euston Road
London NW1 3BH

Franklin Watts Australia
Hachette Children's Books
Level 17/207 Kent Street
Sydney NSW 2000

A CIP catalogue record for this book
is available from the British Library.

Dewey classification number: 341.242'2

ISBN 978 0 7496 6487 9

Printed in China

Franklin Watts is a division of Hachette Children's Books.

Map artwork by Ian Thompson

INSIDE
A1PIX: 3, 26 (bl). Action Press, Rex Features: 26 (cl). AP, Topfoto: 12 (b). Bettmann, Corbis: 11 (tr). Bryan Peterson, Corbis: 23. Charles Bowman, Alamy: 15. Council of the European Union, 2000-2005: 18 (c). Danilo Krstanovic, Reuters, Corbis: 28-29 (tc). Ellie Meddle, Rex Features: 26 (br). Fabrizio Bensch, Reuters, Corbis: 30. Francois Lenoir, Reuters, Corbis: 20. Frederic Sierakowski, Rex Features: 18 (br). Guntmar Fritz, zefa, Corbis: 7. Helen King, Corbis: 24. Hulton-Deutsch Collection, Corbis: 10. KHAM, Reuters, Corbis: 28 (br). Mary Evans Picture Library, Alamy: 11 (br). MXL, Rex Features: 19. Royalty-Free, Corbis: 12 (cl). Sipa Press, Corbis: 6. Sipa Press, Rex Features: 17. Sipa Press, Rex Features: 27. Steve Skjold, Alamy: 25. SXW, Rex Features: 21. Thierry Tronnel, Corbis: 14. Yves Herman, Reuters: 16.

COVER
Front: A1PIX (t). Corbis (bc). Klaus Hackenberg/zefa/Corbis (br). Royalty-Free, Corbis (bl). Back: A1PIX

Contents

What's it all about?

Almost half a billion people live in the European Union (commonly called the EU), making it the world's third-largest population after China (1.3 billion) and India (1 billion).

Twenty-five countries are members of the EU. France has the biggest land area, Germany has the most people and Malta is the smallest on both counts.

The European Union's borders stretch from the freezing cold of the Arctic north to the intense heat of the Mediterranean south, from the Atlantic to the Aegean.

Joining the club

EU members include a unique mix of people, languages, cultures and traditions, who live in a community that wants peace, freedom, prosperity and social justice for everyone.

Every European country can apply for EU membership, but not all want to join. It is a club where the rules are always changing, and people have very different ideas about what the Union is and how it should be run.

Diversity can be the EU's strength. But it can also be its biggest challenge, especially now that 25 nations are competing to get their own voice heard. Each country is trying to juggle their national interests with those of Europe as a whole.

The power of the Union

The European Union is not a federation like the United States, but neither is it only a gathering of countries like the United Nations. In other words, it is not a state that replaces the ones we already have, but it does go further than just international co-operation.

Member states agree to hand over power to the EU on issues where they believe they will have more success and strength working together. However, the EU only has the powers that member countries have chosen to give it.

An EU festival brings together young people from many countries in a spirit of peace and co-operation.

For example, pollution takes no notice of borders, so EU members have agreed common rules that everyone must follow. At least half of all national laws begin life as EU laws.

Individual countries still have the right to choose what to do about issues like defence or foreign policy, but they often act together to pack a bigger punch. For instance, there are now EU peacekeepers in Bosnia.

Striking a deal

The EU's work is based on agreements called treaties. To put them into action, three institutions have been created: the European Parliament, the European Commission and the Council of the European Union. You can find out more about how they work in coming chapters.

Almost every deal is the result of a compromise between the national interests of all the countries in the EU, and those of the three institutions.

Finding friends and allies, rather than confrontation, is how you get things done in the club of 25.

SUPERSIZE EU

When ten new members joined the EU in May 2004, it changed the face of Europe. At a stroke, the EU's surface area increased by one-quarter, its population by one-fifth. In population terms, it became the world's biggest single market. And after years of conflict and division, most of Europe was uniting again in a peaceful way.

The EU flag: 12 stars in a circle, symbolising the ideals of perfection, completeness and unity.

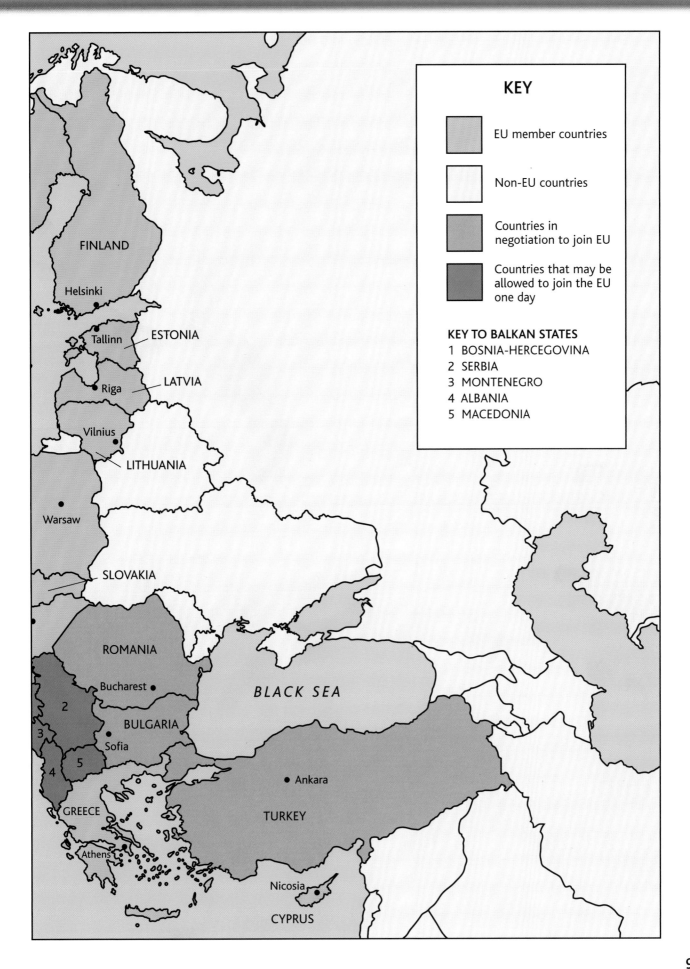

KEY

EU member countries

Non-EU countries

Countries in negotiation to join EU

Countries that may be allowed to join the EU one day

KEY TO BALKAN STATES
1 BOSNIA-HERCEGOVINA
2 SERBIA
3 MONTENEGRO
4 ALBANIA
5 MACEDONIA

FINLAND

Helsinki

Tallinn — ESTONIA

Riga — LATVIA

Vilnius

LITHUANIA

Warsaw

SLOVAKIA

ROMANIA

Bucharest

BLACK SEA

2

BULGARIA

3

Sofia

5

4

Ankara

GREECE

TURKEY

Athens

Nicosia

CYPRUS

History: Part one

The vision of a united Europe rose out of the killing and devastation of two world wars. People were looking for ways of making sure that Europeans would never again be locked in conflict with each other. They dreamed of the end of rivalry and hatred, and the beginning of a new era of peace.

A man with a vision

In 1946, Britain's war-time Prime Minister, Winston Churchill, summed up Europe's challenge:

Dresden, Germany, in 1945. Out of the ashes of war, European nations had to build again.

'Over wide areas a vast quivering mass of tormented, hungry, care-worn and bewildered human beings gape at the ruins of their cities and homes, and scan the dark horizons for the approach of some new peril, tyranny or terror.'

His solution was 'to re-create the European family, or as much of it as we can, and provide it with a structure under which it can dwell in peace, in safety and in freedom. We must build a kind of United States of Europe.'

Sixty years later, the building work still goes on, but Churchill's vision still rings true, with peace, safety and freedom at the heart of the EU project.

TIMELINE

1950: Driven by their dream of peace and prosperity for Europe, the EU's founders spring into action. As a former Assistant Secretary General of the League of Nations, cognac salesman and banker, Jean Monnet knows how to strike deals. He comes up with a plan for Germany and France to pool their production of coal and steel (the two main ingredients for making guns).

The French foreign minister Robert Schuman takes up Monnet's proposal, and announces it on 9 May (the EU's birthday). He says it will make war between Germany and France 'not merely unthinkable, but materially impossible', and invites other nations to join.

1951: The Treaty of Paris establishes the European Coal and Steel Community. Belgium, the Netherlands, Luxembourg and Italy also sign up.

1957: The same six nations agree the Treaty of Rome. They set up the European Economic Community (the EEC), aimed at boosting trade through the free movement of workers, goods, services and money. This will be at the heart of the European adventure. Members also create the European Atomic Energy Authority (Euratom), to help in the peaceful development of nuclear power.

1961: The EEC is a success. The UK, Denmark and Ireland apply to join, but the French President Charles de Gaulle is not impressed, accusing Britain of being too pro-American in its foreign and economic policy: 'Britain neither thinks nor acts like a continental nation, and so is not yet qualified for membership.' He twice vetoes the British application (1963 and 1967).

1967: Three institutions are merged into one to form the European Community (EC).

1973: The UK, Denmark and Ireland are finally allowed to join, after de Gaulle is replaced as president of France. Norway is also offered a place but Norwegian voters say no.

1977: Portugal and Spain join.

1979: The Community plants the seeds of the single currency, the euro, with the introduction of the European Monetary System and a currency unit, the Ecu. And for the first time, members of the European Parliament are democratically elected.

1981: Greece becomes the 10th member.

1985: The President of the European Commission, Jacques Delors, paves the way for a 'single market'. It aims to take away all barriers to free trade or free movement of money or workers. The deadline is 1992. His plan comes after a long period of economic downturn, and fierce debate on what the European project is for, and how to pay for it.

Jean Monnet (1888-1979), the architect of the European Union.

'We are not bringing together states, we are uniting people.'
— Jean Monnet, 1952

French president Charles de Gaulle opposed expansion of the EEC.

History: Part two

In the 1990s, as East and West Germany re-unified and the Soviet Union collapsed, European leaders made plans for changing the face of their continent. There was a new name: the European Community became the European Union. There would be new rights for citizens, new economic freedoms, a new currency, a plan to expand eastwards and an attempt to rewrite the rulebook.

Maastricht paved the way for the new euro currency.

European leaders sign the Maastricht Treaty.

Building for the future

At the core of these changes was a deal signed by EU leaders in 1991, in the modest Dutch town of Maastricht. The famous 'Maastricht Treaty' brought together the EU's three founding treaties. It ushered in a detailed plan for 'Economic and Monetary Union' (EMU), which would lead to countries all using the same currency, the euro.

In Maastricht, heads of state agreed to do more together in areas such as the environment, education, workers' rights, health and safety and research. The EU became more political: it would take joint action on foreign and security matters (the new 'Common Foreign and Security Policy'). There would also be improved co-operation in areas of justice and policing (the 'Justice and Home Affairs' policy), and countries agreed to work together on issues like asylum, immigration, crime, terrorism, drug trafficking and fraud.

TIMELINE

1991: Heads of state sign up to the Maastricht Treaty.

1992/93: European citizens vote in referendums on Maastricht, and many give it a rough ride. In France, it passes only by a 2% margin. In Denmark, voters only approve it second time round. Anti-EU feeling is strong in countries like the UK and Germany.

1995: Austria, Finland and Sweden join the EU. People in Norway once more reject membership. Under the Schengen agreement, France, Germany, Belgium, the Netherlands, Luxembourg, Portugal and Spain end border controls between their nations. Other members (apart from the UK and Ireland) later follow suit.

1997: EU leaders sign the Amsterdam Treaty. One of its main goals is to prepare for enlargement: welcoming a big group of new members into the club. It also makes changes to the way that member states vote, and strengthens laws on issues like employment and discrimination.

1998: The EU begins membership talks with Cyprus, the Czech Republic, Estonia, Hungary, Poland and Slovenia. A year later, it is the turn of Bulgaria, Latvia, Lithuania, Malta, Romania and Slovakia.

2000: The Nice Treaty is agreed. It sets out the rules for an enlarged European Union of 27 members. It also lets groups of countries go ahead faster with some forms of co-operation, for example on defence. In the same year, in Portugal, the EU announces its 'Lisbon Strategy': plans for 'the most competitive and dynamic knowledge-based economy in the world'.

2002: Out go familiar national currencies like the deutschmark and the franc, in comes the euro. On 1 January, euro notes and coins become the official currency for 12 European nations. Sweden, Denmark and the UK strike a deal so that they will not join now, but might join later.

2003: The EU promises the countries of the Balkans that they too will one day become members.

2004: Ten new members join the club on 1 May: eight from the former communist bloc (the Czech Republic, Slovakia, Hungary, Poland, Slovenia, Estonia, Latvia and Lithuania) and two islands in the Mediterranean (Cyprus and Malta). In October, EU leaders sign a new constitution: a set of rules crafted to make the EU easier to understand, and to replace all the existing treaties.

2005: People in France and the Netherlands reject the new constitution in referendums. Several other countries approve the new rules, but they can only come into effect if all 25 nations say yes. Some people warn that this is the end of the road for Europe's first constitution. However, the EU continues with plans to get bigger. It starts membership talks with Croatia and – controversially – with Turkey, the largest and poorest candidate country and the only one with a mainly Muslim population.

2006: The EU carries on its work based on the old rules. With its future direction in doubt, EU leaders consider their next step.

2007 or 2008: Bulgaria and Romania are expected to join.

'From war we have created peace.
From hatred we have created respect.
From division we have created union.
From dictatorship and oppression we have created vibrant and sturdy democracies.
From poverty we have created prosperity.
Our European Union is truly unique.'

FROM THE DECLARATION ON ACCESSION DAY,
DUBLIN, 1 MAY, 2004

The European Commission

Along with the Parliament and the Council, the European Commission was set up in the 1950s under the EU's founding treaties. The Commission manages the daily running of the EU and the spending of EU funds. It proposes new laws and makes sure everyone obeys the rules. If not, it can take rule-breakers to the EU Court of Justice. It is often called the 'guardian of the treaties'.

Triangle of power

The Commission, the Parliament and the Council make up an 'institutional triangle'. National governments have handed over some of their power to these institutions, and expect them to do what is best for the EU as a whole. They are most successful when they all work closely together and trust each other.

The Austrian EU commissioner for external relations, Benita Ferrero-Waldner, makes a point during a press conference in 2005.

COMMISSION FACT SHEET

- It is based in the Belgian capital, Brussels.
- There are twenty-five commissioners, one from each member state.
- National governments put commissioners forward, but their selection has to be approved by Parliament.
- Each commissioner handles a specific area of EU policy, from trade to agriculture.
- He or she needs to look after the interests of the EU as a whole, not just those of their home country.
- There is also a Commission President, chosen from the 25 commissioners by EU member states and approved by the Parliament.
- The President and commissioners serve a five-year term. They are in power at the same time as members of the European Parliament.
- The Commission represents the EU on the world stage.
- Behind the scenes, 24,000 civil servants help the Commission carry out its work. By comparison, twice this number are employed by the council in Birmingham, the UK's second city.

Scandal in the Commission

If Parliament is not happy with the work of the commissioners, it can vote to sack every one of them (but not individuals). This almost happened in 1999, when several commissioners were accused of appointing close friends and of handling funds badly. All the members resigned before the issue came to a vote in Parliament, and the new commissioners promised to make big changes in the way they worked.

LAYING DOWN THE LAW

If member states have agreed that laws enacted by the EU as a whole will mean better results than national governments acting alone, the Commission will be the driving force behind putting those laws into action.

Areas where only the EU passes laws:
- Single market (the same trading rules for everyone)
- Customs (the rules at the EU's external borders)
- Monetary policy (for countries who have signed up to the euro)

Areas where both the EU and member states can pass laws:
- Agriculture and fisheries
- Regional funding
- Environment
- Consumer protection
- Employment and health and safety at work
- Transport
- Energy
- Public health and food safety

(but note that if the EU acts first on one of these, then member states may not pass laws themselves)

Areas where the EU can act but member states keep the right to pass legislation:
- International development
- Research and space policy

Areas where member states have most of the responsibility, but the EU can help:
- Healthcare
- Industry
- Culture
- Tourism
- Education

(For example: the EU will not tell you how to run your local hospital, but it will run campaigns against smoking.)

Situated in Brussels, the EU's Berlaymont building has been specially constructed as a state-of-the-art headquarters for the EU.

The European Parliament

arliament is a melting pot of opinions. It is the place where Europe's elected politicians battle to balance the interests of their country with the interests of Europe as a whole, and decide if proposals from the Commission should become law.

On the move

The European Parliament works in two places. Full meetings for elected Members of the European Parliament (MEPs) are in the French town of Strasbourg for one week every month. The rest of the time there are committees and other meetings in Brussels. This split adds to the running costs and can be unpopular. But for France, the Strasbourg Parliament is a source of national pride. There is another location involved: the people who do the Parliament's administration are based in Luxembourg.

A babble of voices

Making sure everyone understands what is going on in Parliament can be a complicated business. In 2006, there were already 20 different European languages to deal with, and more to come. That means, in theory, at least 190 different language combinations, although in practice interpretation is usually done through English, French and German. There is also the problem of translating more than 100,000 pages of EU rules and regulations, so that British farmers, French fishermen or Polish plumbers can read things in their own language.

French MEPs hold up placards supporting a 'yes' vote during the debate in the run-up to the French vote on the proposed European constitution in 2005. Despite their actions, 55 per cent of French voters rejected the constitution.

THE SEATS OF POWER

Parliament is divided into seven main political groups. None of them has an overall majority, so there is a lot of negotiation needed to get things agreed. Most MEPs belong to one of the main groups, which cover the political spectrum from left to right. They get funding and committee posts according to their size.

Political make-up of the Parliament chosen in the 2004 elections

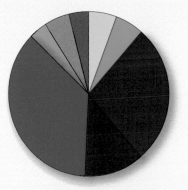

- European United Left/Nordic Green Left (EU/NGL) – far left parties, 41 seats
- Greens/European Free Alliance (EFA) – Greens and regionalists/nationalists – 42 seats
- Party of European Socialists (PES) (includes British Labour party) – 200 seats
- Alliance of Liberals and Democrats for Europe – Liberals/Centrists – 88 seats
- European People's Party and European Democrats (EPP-ED) – 268 seats
- Union for Europe of the Nations (UEN) – Right-wing/Gaullists – 27 seats
- Independence and Democracy (IND/DEM) – Eurosceptics – 37 seats
- MEPs unattached to any group (NA) – 29 seats

This picture shows MEPs voting during a session of the European Parliament in Strasbourg.

PARLIAMENT FACT SHEET

- The people of Europe vote for members of Parliament every five years. The last poll was in June 2004.
- If you are an EU citizen and over 18, you can vote in the elections. That is the case wherever you live in the EU.
- There are 732 MEPs from all 25 EU countries. About one-third are women.
- When the Commission comes up with proposals for new laws, members of Parliament perform their main job – deciding whether to pass those laws.
- They debate and vote on issues like the economy, immigration, health, consumer protection and the environment. They are also responsible for approving the EU's annual budget.
- Proposed laws can be thrown out if a majority of MEPs vote against them.
- Parliament shares these decision-making powers with the Council of the European Union: this is called 'co-decision'. A law can only pass if both bodies approve it.
- MEPs also supervise other EU institutions, like the Commission.
- The Parliament has a president who serves for two-and-a-half years.

The Council of the European Union

The Council is where the governments of Europe are represented, and the big decisions are made. The Council shares responsibility with Parliament for passing laws and approving budgets. But in an EU club that keeps getting bigger, its leaders often struggle to agree on important issues.

British Prime Minister Tony Blair (left) signs the Accession Treaty on 16 April 2003. This treaty allowed the EU to expand in 2004.

Which council is which?

The Council of the European Union (also known as the Council of Ministers) Ministers from each EU country meet here, to take decisions and pass laws. Who shows up depends on what is being discussed. If it is about health, for example, the health minister attends. Most meetings are in Brussels.

The European Council These are the high-profile summit meetings attended by presidents and prime ministers. The European Council meets four times a year, and may try to settle key issues that their ministers have not been able to agree on. Trying to strike deals between 25 different countries, with widely different opinions, is often tricky.

Franco Frattini, then Vice-President of the European Council, presides at a justice and home affairs meeting in Brussels, 2005.

Asylum seekers in a French detention centre. Asylum and immigration is one of the many issues dealt with by the Council.

Taking a vote

If the Council is tackling a sensitive issue – like taxation, asylum, immigration, foreign policy or defence – every one of the member countries must agree. In fact, EU ministers and leaders rarely vote at all, as they find it is too divisive. They prefer to do things by consensus. On other topics, though, decisions are usually made by a system known as 'qualified majority voting'. This means:

- The biggest countries get the most votes. So France, Germany, Italy and Britain, for example, have 29 votes each out of a total of 321. Smaller nations get fewer.

- There must be at least 232 votes in favour, cast by more than half of the member countries.

- Under plans for a new EU constitution, the voting system would be made simpler.

Sharing the power

Each six months, a new EU country takes a turn at holding the presidency of the EU. This means chairing meetings like the Council summits, and representing the EU on the international stage.

JUST TO CONFUSE YOU: THE COUNCIL OF EUROPE...

...is *not* an EU institution. It was set up in 1949, before the EU was founded. There are 46 members and its purpose is to defend and promote human rights, the rule of law and democracy throughout Europe. In particular, it has been a watchdog on human rights in countries that broke away from the Soviet Union. Its most important ruling is the European Convention on Human Rights. If an EU citizen has run out of options on a case in their country, they can take it to the Court of Human Rights in Strasbourg.

The rule of law

If a member state does not like a new EU law that has been passed, it cannot simply ignore it. That new law takes precedence over existing national rules, because that is what countries sign up to when they join the EU. Here are some of the bodies that try to give everyone in the EU a fair deal.

A Danish judge presides at a hearing in the EU Court of Justice in Luxembourg.

LAW AND THE EU

THE COURT OF JUSTICE

- It makes sure that EU member states and institutions do what the law requires them to do, equally for everyone, respecting the fundamental rights of EU citizens.
- It checks that national courts do not give different rulings on the same issue.
- If called upon by a member state, the Court of Justice can give rulings on how to interpret EU law. For example, the French government banned imports of British beef: the European Court said this broke EU rules and ordered France to follow them.
- The Court of Justice is based in Luxembourg. There is one judge from each EU country, serving a term of six years.

THE COURT OF AUDITORS

- The EU is funded by money from taxpayers, so the Court of Auditors tries to make sure they are getting value for money.
- The Court of Auditors is based in Luxembourg, and can audit any organisation, body or company that handles EU money.
- There is one member from each EU country, serving a six-year term.

THE EUROPEAN ECONOMIC AND SOCIAL AFFAIRS COMMITTEE

- This is known as the 'voice of civil society'. It is an advisory body with 317 members representing a wide range of interests, from employers to trade unions, from consumers to ecologists.
- It must be consulted about decisions on economic and social matters.

THE COMMITTEE OF THE REGIONS

- Its 317 members are often leaders of regional government, or mayors of cities.
- They are consulted when EU decisions are going to have a big impact on people regionally, for example, on transport or health.

THE OMBUDSMAN

- The Ombudsman is an independent go-between for complaints brought by individuals against EU authorities.
- Citizens of the EU can turn to the Ombudsman if they think an EU body has acted unfairly.
- The Ombudsman considers issues such as discrimination, abuse of power, lack of information or refusal to give it, or unnecessary delays in resolving outstanding issues.

The EU and football: a landmark case

The Union's lawmakers have had a big influence on the world of European football. When Belgian footballer Jean-Marc Bosman won a case against his club FC Liége at the European Court of Justice in 1995, it revolutionised football across Europe. Before the Bosman ruling, clubs demanded a transfer fee when a player moved from one club to another, even if that player's contract had finished. But this was against EU employment law, because it restricted a person's freedom of movement. So now, when footballers' contracts have run out, they have the right to move to another club on a 'Bosman free transfer'.

Getting your voice heard

Along with the bigger courts, there may be another road to justice if you are an EU citizen worried about a day-to-day local issue: the Petitions Committee of the European Parliament. For example, it took up the case of a Polish baker who moved to a German town but could not set up a business there, because ancient laws allowed only a maximum of three bakers. After pressure from this EU committee, the German government changed the rules.

England international Sol Campbell: under the Bosman ruling, Arsenal signed him for free from their rivals Tottenham, instead of paying a big transfer fee.

Money

Money makes the EU's world go round. Striving for a strong economy is at the heart of everything the Union has achieved, and aims to achieve in the future. It wants higher standards of living for its people, because it believes that with prosperity comes peace. And since 2002, the EU has had a symbol of its economic ambitions: the euro.

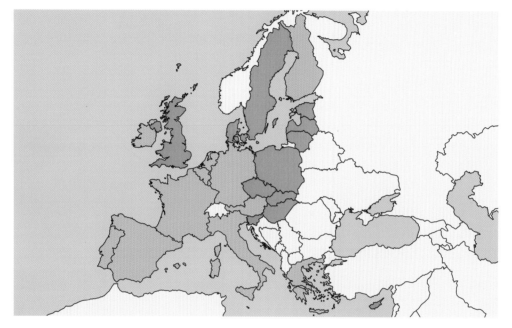

WHO USES THE EURO?

EU countries using the euro (the 'eurozone')

EU member states not using the euro; some will join the eurozone at a future date.

Who's in, who's out

IN: Austria, Belgium, Finland, France, Germany, Greece, Ireland, Italy, Luxembourg, the Netherlands, Portugal, Spain.

OUT: The UK and Denmark have agreed a deal where they can decide to join the eurozone at a later stage. The British government says it is in favour of joining in principle, if economic conditions are right. Sweden's voters rejected euro membership in a referendum in 2003.

WAITING: When the ten new member states joined the EU in 2004, they committed to using the euro. Earliest likely date: 2007.

One of the EU's most striking achievements is the single currency because:

• It is a world currency that makes trade easier between the nations that use it

• It allows people to travel throughout Europe without having to change money

• It is a symbol of the EU's political progress

THE EUROPEAN CENTRAL BANK: KEY FACTS

• It is based in Frankfurt, Germany.
• It was set up in 1998 to introduce and manage the euro.
• It decides on interest rates across the euro area.
• It aims to keep inflation below 2%.
• It is entirely independent of other EU institutions or national governments.
• It is responsible for shaping and managing monetary and economic policy.
• Its decisions are made by the Governing Council: an Executive Board plus governors of 12 central banks from the euro area.

Dishing out the money

In 2005, the EU had more than 100 billion euros to spend – that is about 1% of the gross national income of its members.

A large portion was for foreign aid and foreign policy (8 bn euros), administration (6 bn), research (4 bn) and other spending (7 bn)

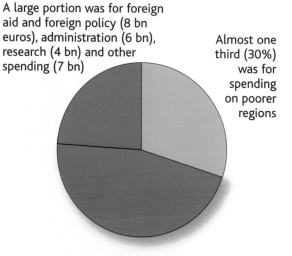

Almost one third (30%) was for spending on poorer regions

Almost half (46%) was for aid to farmers and rural development

The euro has become a powerful symbol of what the EU stands for.

THE EUROPEAN INVESTMENT BANK

- It lends money at very low rates to countries in the EU and in the former Soviet Union and Mediterranean region.
- Money can be used for projects like roads, bridges, water purification plants.
- It is based in Luxembourg.

MORE KEY FACTS

- The EU is expected to spend a total of 862.36 bn euros over seven years, between 2007-2013. That is 1.045% of the EU's combined gross national income.
- How much you give to the EU budget depends on how big your economy is: you generally get the most cash out of it if you are poorer than the average.
- In 2004, Germany paid in the most and received the least in return ('net contribution'). Spain was at the opposite end of the scale.

Agriculture

Only about 5% of people across the EU work in farming, and it accounts for only 1.6% of the EU's GDP. Yet spending on agriculture makes up almost half the budget and it is an issue that still causes furious rows among member states. Why?

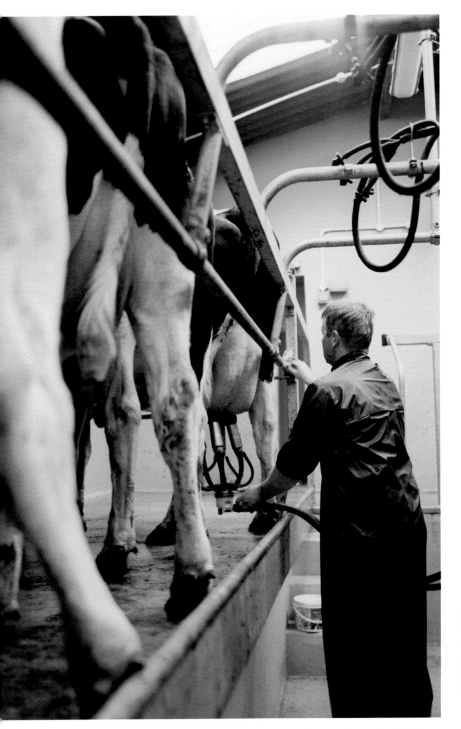

A dairy farmer milks his herd. Some EU members get less than half the agricultural subsidies paid to others.

Does the 'CAP' fit?

The answer lies in the deal that was made in the EU's early days. France agreed to a free trade in industrial goods among the six founder members, but only if its farmers were given subsidies – extra money to make sure they had a good income.

The agreement is known as the 'Common Agricultural Policy' (CAP). It came into play in 1962, when people still had strong memories of wartime food shortages, and wanted to avoid the same thing happening again.

This is how the CAP worked: the European Community set a target price for farm goods. If the market price dropped lower, it would step in and pay the extra. But as the years went by farmers kept on producing more and more, because they knew they would get a good price for it.

This led to notorious 'mountains' and 'lakes' of food and drink that no one wanted, but that member states still had to pay for in subsidies. Also, Europe's food prices have been some of the highest in the world.

CAP'S AIMS:
- To make farms more productive
- To ensure fair living standards for the agricultural community
- To stabilise markets
- To ensure food is available
- To provide food at reasonable prices (from the Treaty of Rome).

Changing direction

There has been a lot of talk about reforming CAP, but change only really began in the 1990s and it is still going slowly. One of the main aims has been to give more aid to farmers for things like food safety, animal welfare and looking after the environment, rather than for how much they produce.

Critics of CAP say it is much too expensive and only benefits a minority of people. Supporters argue that it helps rural communities, where more than half of EU citizens live. They say it also preserves the traditional look of the countryside.

This is how the EU shared out CAP funds in 2004:

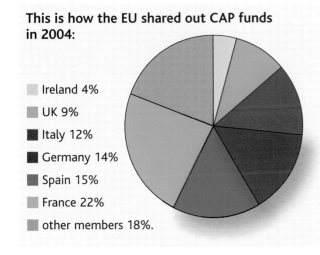

- Ireland 4%
- UK 9%
- Italy 12%
- Germany 14%
- Spain 15%
- France 22%
- other members 18%.

Facts about farming

- Most of the CAP money has been going to the biggest farmers: as of 2004, about 80% of the funds went to just 20% of EU farmers...

- ... and 40% of farmers shared only 8% of the funds.

- The new member states began to get CAP funds in 2004. But they were given only one-quarter of the money paid to older EU members. This will rise gradually and the share is due to become equal in 2013.

- Poland has the biggest proportion of farmers in the EU – 2.5 million, or 16% of the population.

- Across the EU, 2% of farmers leave the business every year. The average age of a farmer is 55 years, and rising.

Harvest in progress at Zawady, central Poland. The newest member states will see their CAP subsidies rise to eventually match those of the older EU members.

The EU and its citizens

Most people would agree that life in Europe has become more prosperous and peaceful in the years since the EU began, although not everyone would agree that this is mainly because of the EU.

According to an official 'Eurobarometer' survey in autumn 2004, about 56% of people across the 25 nations say the EU is 'a good thing'. People in Luxembourg (85%) believe in it the most, people in the UK (38%) the least.

Getting closer, but keeping a distance

For some people, the EU can still seem like a big, remote, confusing organisation, where governments and experts make plans that have little to do with their everyday lives.

So the challenge for the EU is to strike a balance. It needs to be an effective organisation that makes the best use of its powers, but still lets people in each member state feel unique.

Polish migrant workers in Germany. EU citizens have the right to move to – and work in – other countries of the Union.

SYMBOLS OF CITIZENSHIP

Flag: five-pointed stars in a crown. There are 12 stars, a number representing perfection and completeness.

Passport: 'European Union' is written at the top, the name of the member state follows. It is burgundy red and the same size for everyone.

Anthem: Beethoven's Ninth Symphony, with the words of Schiller's 'Ode to Joy'.

Birthday: Europe Day is on 9 May, to mark the birthdate of Robert Schuman, one of the the main founders of the EU (see page 11).

Driving licence: you can drive anywhere in the EU if you have a licence from one of the member states.

KNOWING YOUR RIGHTS

If you live in an EU country, you are a citizen of the European Union, and these are some of your basic rights:

- You can move freely between EU countries, and live in any EU nation you choose.
- From the age of 18, you can vote and stand in local government and European Parliament elections in the country where you live.
- You can receive health care, social security and social assistance throughout the EU.
- If you believe the EU has not been fair to you, you can take your case to the European Ombudsman.

FROM 'GOODBYE BENDY BANANAS' TO 'TOYS FOR PIGS'

The media in Eurosceptic nations like the UK are fond of finding headlines that suggest the bureaucrats of Brussels are ruling people's lives with crazy new laws.

According to stories in the London *Times* newspaper, for instance, the EU was going to ban bananas or cucumbers that were too bendy, and make farmers give toys to their pigs to keep them happy.

The EU says the media often get the facts wrong, and devotes a whole corner of its official website to correcting mistakes. Bendy bananas and strict pig farmers, it says, are not in their sights.

The EU and the world

The European Union wants to play a leading role on the world stage, and wherever it can it tries to speak with one voice. But while the EU is a force to be reckoned with in the global economy, it has much less impact on world politics. So some critics call it 'an economic giant but a political dwarf'.

It also lacks a figurehead in the form of a leader who can tell the world what the EU thinks. As US diplomat Henry Kissinger famously asked in the 1970s: 'If I want to talk to Europe, who do I phone?'

Troops stand to attention in Sarajevo at a ceremony to mark the handover of Balkan peacekeeping duties from NATO to an EU force in December 2004.

The EU Trade Commissioner poses with his Vietnamese counterpart to announce Vietnam's inclusion in the World Trade Organization, October 2004.

TRADING UP

- The EU is the world's largest free-trade area, and accounts for about one-fifth of global imports and exports.
- The EU gives more than half of the world's development aid.
- The EU's trade ties with the United States are the broadest and deepest of any in the world: between 2000-2005, three-quarters of the EU's foreign investment went to the US, and more than half of America's came to the EU.
- Every day, transatlantic trade is worth at least one billion dollars, and means jobs for six million Americans and Europeans.
- The EU is one of China's top trading partners, and business is growing.
- The EU keeps close links with its former colonies: countries in Africa, the Caribbean and the Pacific (known as the ACP). Seventy-nine countries are now in the ACP, and between 2003 and 2008 they were in line to get $16 billion in aid.

Talking business

Unity is easier in matters of trade, because member states have handed over all their negotiating powers to the EU Commission. They believe they will get the best deal if they stick together.

At meetings of the World Trade Organisation, for example, the EU says its aim is to push for fair and equal access to markets around the world, and to persuade others to stick to the rules. However, critics say that the EU's own rules on protecting its farmers get in the way of free trade.

Talking politics

For the EU, it can be difficult to speak with one voice on issues like defence and foreign policy. That is because member states have kept the right to decide these issues for themselves, and often disagree on what to do. There were big disputes, for example, over the invasion of Iraq in 2003.

In 1999, the EU appointed Javier Solana, a former secretary general of NATO, as its first foreign policy chief. He is the man meant to speak for Europe on international affairs. But he only has something to say when all the 25 EU governments agree, so he had to stay silent during the Iraq crisis.

The backbone of the EU's approach to world affairs is the Common Foreign and Security Policy (CFSP). It deals with issues like peace, security, international co-operation, democracy, human rights and rule of law.

EU leaders do find common cause wherever they can. The EU holds regular summit meetings with other big countries or world organisations like the United Nations. It tries to strike deals on key world issues, from poverty to terrorism. The EU is one of the 'Quartet', along with the United States, Russia and the United Nations, trying to bring peace to the Middle East.

Taking stock

The world has never seen a political project as grand and bold as the European Union. It is unique for so many nation-states to hand over so much of their sovereignty.

The EU itself has many of the symbols of a nation: it has a flag, an anthem, a currency and a single market. It keeps expanding both its size and its ambitions. As it tries to come up with more common policy on foreign and security affairs, it will look even more like a single nation.

Knowing who you are

Each country still keeps much of what makes it unique. The French have not become less French because they are in the EU, and neither have the British become less British.

A lot is still decided by how the big countries in Western Europe – Britain, France and Germany – get along. But countries in Eastern Europe, like Poland, are playing a more and more important role.

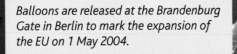
Balloons are released at the Brandenburg Gate in Berlin to mark the expansion of the EU on 1 May 2004.

The EU's institutions in action

EUROPEAN COMMISSION

approves and supervises the Commission

appoints members of the Commission

comes up with proposals for new laws

EUROPEAN PARLIAMENT

COUNCIL OF THE EU

citizens vote for 732 MEPs

jointly agree

ministers are from national government

EU LAW

COURT OF JUSTICE

makes sure law is applied, gives verdict in case of disputes

So where now for the EU?

The questions that will challenge the European Union of the future are the same ones that have puzzled it in the past. How much power do member states want to hand over to the EU, and how can they reach agreement when there are so many different points of view?

Such questions are at the heart of every dispute, on everything from a 'yes-or-no' vote on the EU constitution, to a battle over whether a Polish plumbing business is allowed to offer the same services in Paris as it does in Warsaw.

Even when there is a verdict on an issue, it is rarely a simple one, and different people read it in different ways, depending on where their interest lies.

So a unique project like the European Union is both fascinating and confusing, and its activities will continue to fascinate and confuse people for years to come.

FRANCE

Capital: Paris

Population: 60.7 million

Population growth rate: 0.37%

Average age: 38.85 years

Life expectancy at birth: 79.6 years (male 75.96 years, female 83.42 years)

Total land area: 543, 965 sq km (the largest in Western Europe)

Border countries: Andorra, Belgium, Germany, Italy, Luxembourg, Monaco, Spain, Switzerland

Coastline: 3,427 km

Religions: Roman Catholic 83-88%, Protestant 2%, Jewish 1%, Muslim 5-10%, unaffiliated 4%

Government type: republic: presidential democracy. President elected by popular vote every five years. A bicameral (two-chamber) parliament is made up of the Senate and National Assembly. The President names the Prime Minister

Administration: France has 22 metropolitan regions (including Corsica) and four overseas regions, made up of islands and territories in other continents. These (French Guiana, Guadeloupe, Martinique, Reunion) are part of the French Republic, but not part of the EU

Economy: government has majority ownership of railways, electricity, aircraft and telecommunications but is loosening its control

GDP: $1.816 trillion, made up of agriculture 2.5%, industry 21.4%, and services 76.1%

Industries: aircraft, machinery, chemicals, automobiles, metals, electronics; textiles, food processing; tourism

Labour force: 27.72 million

Unemployment: 10%

Currency: euro

Calling code: +33

Language: French. There are also several regional languages

France in the EU: a founder member (Treaty of Rome 1957); 78 MEPs, 1 commissioner, Europe's most ethnically diverse country; French voted 'no' in a referendum on the EU Constitution in 2005

France in the world: a founding member of the UN; one of the five permanent members of the UN Security Council; one of only eight acknowledged nuclear powers; NATO member; fifth-largest world economy in 2004; world's number one tourist destination in 2003 with 75 million visitors

GERMANY

Capital: Berlin

Population: 82.5 million (the largest in the EU)

Population growth rate: 0%

Average age: 42.16 years (male 40.88 years, female 43.53 years)

Life expectancy at birth: 78.65 years (male 75.66 years, female 81.81 years)

Total land area: 357,027 sq km

Border countries: Denmark, Poland, Czech Republic, Austria, Switzerland, France, Luxembourg, Belgium, the Netherlands (more than any other European country)

Coastline: 2,389 km

Religions: Protestant 34%, Catholic 34%, Muslim 3.7%, unaffiliated 28.3%

Ethnic groups: German 91.5%, Turkish 2.4%, other 6.1%

Government type: federal republic, parliamentary democracy. The power is divided between the federation and the 16 individual states. A bicameral parliament is made up of the Federal Assembly (Bundestag) and the Federal Council (Bundesrat)

Economy: Europe's largest, but has grown slowly in recent years. Germany's population is ageing, and unemployment is high. Integrating with East Germany has been a challenge

GDP: $2.446 trillion, made up of agriculture 1.1%, industry 28.6%, services 70.3%

Exports: machinery, vehicles, chemicals, metals, foodstuffs, consumer electronics, textiles, electricity. One of the world's largest producers of iron, steel, cement, chemicals, machinery, motor vehicles, machine tools, electronics

Labour force: 43.32 million

Unemployment: 11.6%

Currency: euro

Calling code: +49

Language: German. There are also minor regional languages

Germany in the EU: a founder member; 99 MEPs (largest number); Europe's most populous nation and most powerful economy; East and West Germany reunified in 1990

Germany in the world: one of the leading industrialised nations; member state of UN, NATO, G8; pushing for permanent membership of UN Security Council

ITALY

Capital: Rome

Population: 57.2 million

Population growth rate: 0.07%

Average age: 41.77 years
(male 40.24 years, female 43.35 years)

Life expectancy at birth: 79.68 years
(male 76.75 years, female 82.81 years)

Total land area: 301,338 sq km

Border countries: Austria, France, Holy See
(Vatican City), San Marino, Slovenia, Switzerland

Coastline: 7,600 km

Religions: 87% Catholic, 13% other or
unaffiliated. Growing Muslim population

Government type: democratic republic. Bicameral
parliament consisting of Chamber of Deputies and
Senate. There is a separate judiciary and an
executive branch with a Council of Ministers
(cabinet) headed by the Prime Minister. The
President of the Republic is elected for seven
years, and nominates the Prime Minister. Several
dozen governments since World War II

Administration: 20 regions; five have special
autonomous status

Economy: industrial north with many private
companies. South is more dependent on welfare
and agriculture, and there is high unemployment
(20%)

GDP: $1.645 trillion, made up of agriculture 2.1%,
industry 28.8%, services 69.1%

Industries: tourism, machinery, chemicals, iron
and steel, food processing, textiles, motor
vehicles, clothing, footwear, ceramics

Labour force: 24.49 million

Unemployment: 7.9%

Currency: euro

Calling code: +39

Languages: Italian. French, German and Slovene
spoken in some areas, and many dialects

Italy in the EU: a founder member; 78 MEPs

Italy in the world: rich cultural history and home
to largest number of UNESCO World Heritage
sites (40); NATO member; long coastline is
magnet for illegal immigrants from North Africa
and southeast Europe

THE NETHERLANDS

Capital: Amsterdam

Population: 16.3 million

Population growth rate: 0.53%

Average age: 39.04 years

Life expectancy at birth: 78.81 years
(male 76.25 years, female 81.51 years)

Total land area: 41,526 sq km
(of which almost 20% is water)

Border countries: Belgium and Germany

Coastline: 451 km

Religions: Roman Catholic 31%, Dutch Reformed
13%, Calvinist 7%, Muslim 5.5%, other 2.5%,
none 41%

Ethnic groups: Dutch 83%, other 17% (of which
9% were from non-Western countries including
former Dutch colonies)(1999 estimate)

Government type: constitutional monarchy,
government based in the Hague. The monarch is
the head of state and formally appoints the
government, which is historically always a
coalition because no single party has enough
support to take charge. The Prime Minister heads
the government. Parliament consists of two
houses: the First and Second Chamber

Administration: 12 provinces

Economy: a modern industrialised nation; exports
a large number of agricultural products; a
European transport hub

GDP: $500 billion, made up of agriculture 2.1%,
industry 24.4%, services 73.5%

Industries: mostly food processing, chemicals,
petroleum refining, electrical machinery; has one
of the world's largest natural gas fields; modern
farming system

Labour force: 7.53 million

Unemployment: 6.7%

Currency: euro

Calling code: +31

Languages: Dutch, Frisian

The Netherlands in the EU: founder member; 27
MEPs; Dutch voted 'no' in a referendum on the EU
Constitution in 2005

The Netherlands in the world: often known as
Holland, although this is the name of a region in
the west of the country; one of the world's most
densely populated, flattest and low lying nations
(the name means 'low country'); NATO member;
famous for windmills, dykes, tulips, clogs and
liberal views on drugs and prostitution; hosts the
International Court of Justice

BELGIUM

Capital: Brussels

Population: 10.3 million

Population growth rate: 0.15%

Average age: 40.55 years

Life expectancy at birth: 78.62 years (male 75.44 years, female 81.94 years)

Total land area: 30,528 sq km

Border countries: France, Germany, Luxembourg, the Netherlands

Coastline: 66.5 km

Ethnic groups: Fleming 58%, Walloon 31%, mixed or other 11%

Religions: Roman Catholic 75%, Protestant or other 25%

Government type: federal parliamentary democracy under a constitutional monarch. The King is head of state and formally appoints the Prime Minister and the cabinet. A bicameral parliament consists of a Senate and a Chamber of Deputies. There are now three levels of government (federal, regional and linguistic community) with a complex share of power. Belgium is one of the few countries where, by law, people must vote, so turnout in elections is high

Administration: 10 provinces and 3 regions (Flanders, Wallonia and Brussels)

Economy: one of the most highly industrialised places in the world; few natural resources; Belgium has a modern transport network; about 75% of its trade is with other EU countries

GDP: $329.3 billion, made up of agriculture 1.3%, industry 24.7%, services 74%

Industries: engineering and metal products, motor vehicle assembly, transport equipment, scientific instruments, processed food and drink, chemicals, basic metals, textiles, glass, petroleum

Labour force: 4.77 million

Unemployment: 7.6%

Currency: euro

Calling code: +32

Languages: bilingual: Dutch 60%, French 40%, German (official) less than 1%

Belgium in the EU: at the crossroads of Western Europe; most West European capitals are within 1,000 km of Brussels; 24 MEPs

Belgium in the world: famous for being the home of both the European Union and NATO, for its huge numbers of international diplomats and bureaucrats, and for its chocolate and beer

LUXEMBOURG

Capital: Luxembourg

Population: 465,000

Population growth rate: 1.25%

Average age: 38.51 years

Life expectancy at birth: 78.74 years (male 75.45 years, female 82.24 years)

Total land area: 2,586 sq km

Border countries: Belgium, France, Germany

Coastline: 0 km (landlocked)

Ethnic groups: Celtic base (with French and German blend), Portuguese, Italian, Slavs (from Montenegro, Albania and Kosovo) and European (guest and resident workers)

Religions: 87% Roman Catholic, 13% Protestants, Jews and Muslims

Government type: parliamentary, with a constitutional monarchy. A cabinet of ministers is recommended by the Prime Minister and appointed by the monarch, the Grand Duke. Parliament consists of the Chamber of Deputies

Administration: the Grand Duchy of Luxembourg is made up of three districts

Economy: people in Luxembourg have the highest standard of living in the world (per capita income is $62,700). The economy was once dominated by steel manufacturing but today Luxembourg is best known as a tax haven and a centre for banking

GDP: $29.37 billion, made up of agriculture 0.5%, industry 16.3%, services 83.1%

Industries: banking, iron and steel, food processing, chemicals, metal products, engineering, tyres, glass, aluminium, information technology, tourism

Labour force: 200,000; about 105,000 commute from France, Belgium and Germany

Unemployment: 3.7%

Currency: euro

Calling code: +352

Languages: Luxembourgish (national language). German and French (administrative languages)

Luxembourg in the EU: one of the smallest countries in Europe; a founder member of the EU, and entered into the 'Benelux Customs Union' with Belgium and the Netherlands in 1948

Luxembourg in the world: founder member of NATO, famous for its financial and political stability

DENMARK

Capital: Copenhagen
Population: 5.4 million
Population growth rate: 0.34%
Average age: 39.47 years
Life expectancy at birth: 77.62 years (male 75.34 years, female 80.03 years)
Total land area: 43,094 sq km
Border countries: Germany
Coastline: 7,314 km

Ethnic groups: Scandinavian, Inuit, Faroese, German, Turkish, Iranian, Somali

Religions: Evangelical Lutheran 95%, other Protestant and Roman Catholic 3%, Muslim 2%

Government type: the Kingdom of Denmark is a constitutional monarchy, with a parliament called the People's Assembly. The monarch is the chief of state, and formally appoints the Prime Minister, who appoints a cabinet

Administration: 13 counties and three municipalities. Counties are to be replaced by regions in 2007. The Faroe Islands and Greenland are part of the Kingdom of Denmark, but are self-governing overseas administrative divisions

Economy: very modern. Agriculture is high-tech, and the country is able to export more food and energy than it imports. Good welfare system

GDP: $182.1 billion, made up of agriculture 2.2%, industry 24%, services 73.8%

Industries: iron, steel, chemicals, textiles and clothing, food processing, machinery, transport equipment, electronics, construction, furniture, shipbuilding and refurbishment, windmills

Labour force: 2.9 million

Unemployment: 5.7%

Currency: krone

Calling code: +45

Language: Danish; others: Faroese, Greenlandic (an Inuit dialect), German (small minority), and English is main second language

Denmark in the EU: joined in 1973; 14 MEPs; Denmark chose not to sign up to some parts of the Maastricht Treaty; in September 2000, Danish people voted against making the euro the national currency

Denmark in the world: modern prosperous country; founder member of NATO; when a Danish newspaper published a cartoon depicting the Prophet Muhammad, it sparked worldwide protests by Muslims in 2006

IRELAND

Capital: Dublin
Population: 4 million
Population growth rate: 1.16%
Average age: 33.7 years
Life expectancy at birth: 77.56 years (male 74.95 years, female 80.34 years)
Total land area: 70,182 sq km
Border countries: UK
Coastline: 1,448 km

Religions: Roman Catholic 88.4%, Church of Ireland 3%, other Christian 1.6%, other 1.5%, unspecified 2%, none 3.5%

Government type: parliamentary democracy; bicameral parliament consists of the Senate and the House of Representatives; chief of state is the President

Administration: 26 counties

Economy: has changed from a country that relied mainly on farming, to become a modern, high-tech Celtic Tiger, with impressive economic growth in recent years

GDP: $136.9 billion, made up of agriculture 5%, industry 46%, services 49%

Industries: metal processing; food products, brewing, textiles, clothing; chemicals, pharmaceuticals; machinery, transport equipment, shipping, glass and crystal, software, tourism

Labour force: 2.03 million

Unemployment: 4.2%

Currency: euro

Calling code: +353

Languages: English; Irish Gaelic spoken mainly in western areas

Ireland in the EU: joined in 1973; 13 MEPs; covers five-sixths of the island of Ireland: the rest is known as Northern Ireland and is part of the United Kingdom

Ireland in the world: famous for literature and music; often referred to as the 'Republic of Ireland', to distinguish it from the island of Ireland as a whole; Irish and UK governments worked closely together to reach a peace settlement for Northern Ireland in 1998, after decades of conflict between those who wanted a united Ireland, and those who wanted to stay in the United Kingdom

UNITED KINGDOM

Capital: London

Population: 60.4 million

Population growth rate: 0.28%

Average age: 38.99 years

Life expectancy at birth: 78.38 years (male 75.94 years, female 80.96 years)

Total land area: 244,820 sq km

Border countries: Ireland

Coastline: 12,429 km

Religions: Christian (Anglican, Roman Catholic, Presbyterian, Methodist) 71.6%, Muslim 2.7%, Hindu 1%, other 1.6%, unspecified or none 23.1% (2001 census)

Government type: constitutional monarchy. The monarch is the chief of state. The Houses of Parliament are made up of the House of Lords and the House of Commons. There has been a major move towards devolution of powers to Wales, Scotland and Northern Ireland

Administration: the United Kingdom of Great Britain and Northern Ireland (often called simply 'Britain') is made up of the three countries of England, Wales and Scotland on the island of Great Britain, and the province of Northern Ireland on the island of Ireland. The UK also has several overseas territories

Economy: one of the world's largest. Once driven by manufacturing, now global banking. There is a highly efficient agricultural system and large reserves of coal, natural gas and oil. The UK has not yet adopted the euro as its national currency and debate continues

GDP: $1.867 trillion (2005 est.), made up of agriculture 1.1%, industry 26%, services 72.9%

Industries: transport, power, electronics and communications equipment, vehicles, metals and chemicals, petroleum, paper products, food processing, textiles, clothing, consumer goods

Labour force: 30.07 million

Unemployment: 4.7%

Currency: pound sterling

Calling code: +44

Languages: English, Welsh (spoken by about 26% of the population of Wales), Scottish Gaelic, Irish, Scots, Cornish

UK in the EU: joined in 1973; 78 MEPs; known for a high level of Euroscepticism

UK in the world: NATO member; a permanent member of the UN Security Council. The British Empire once stretched over one-quarter of the Earth

GREECE

Capital: Athens

Population: 11 million

Population growth rate: 0.19%

Average age: 40.5 years

Life expectancy at birth: 79.09 years (male 76.59 years, female 81.76 years)

Total land area: 131,940 sq km

Border countries: Albania, Bulgaria, Turkey, Macedonia

Coastline: 13,676 km

Ethnic groups: Greek 98%, other 2%

Religions: Greek Orthodox 98%, Muslim 1.3%, other 0.7%

Government type: parliamentary republic; unicameral parliament; chief of state is the President

Administration: 13 regions divided into 51 prefectures and 1 autonomous region

Economy: based on shipping (world leader) and tourism (15% of GDP). Many people still work for the state: the public sector makes up about 40% of GDP. Immigrants are nearly one-fifth of the work force (the majority come from neighbouring Albania)

GDP: $242.8 billion, made up of agriculture 6.2%, industry 22.1%, services 71.7%

Industries: tourism, food and tobacco processing, textiles, chemicals, metal products; mining, petroleum

Labour force: 4.72 million

Unemployment: 10.8%

Currency: euro

Calling code: +30

Language: Greek

Greece in the EU: joined in 1981; receives a big slice of EU's aid budget

Greece in the world: many people call it the cradle of civilisation, the birthplace of democracy. Has a rich historical and cultural heritage: Greece's literature, philosophy, art and politics are famous throughout the world. Long history of disputes with neighbour Turkey over territory in the Aegean and the divided island of Cyprus. NATO member. Greece hosted the Olympic Games in 2004

SPAIN

Capital: Madrid

Population: 44.1 million

Population growth rate: 0.15%

Average age: 39.51 years

Life expectancy at birth: 79.52 years (male 76.18 years, female 83.08 years)

Total land area: 505,988 sq km

Border countries: Andorra, France, Gibraltar, Portugal, Morocco

Coastline: 4,964 km

Religions: Roman Catholic 94%, other 6%

Government type: parliamentary monarchy; the monarch is the chief of state; the bicameral National Assembly consists of the Senate and the Congress of Deputies

Administration: 17 autonomous communities and 2 autonomous cities, based on 1978 constitution aimed at protecting linguistic and cultural diversity. But in the Basque region in the north, the separatist group ETA has used violence to push for independence

Economy: modern industrial economy with thriving tourism sector

GDP: $1.014 trillion, made up of agriculture 3.4%, industry 28.7%, services 67.9%

Industries: textiles, clothing, footwear, food and drink, metal and chemicals, shipbuilding, cars, tourism, pharmaceuticals, medical equipment

Labour force: 20.67 million

Unemployment: 10.1%

Currency: euro

Calling code: +34

Languages: Castilian Spanish 74%, Catalan 17%, Galician 7%, Basque 2%. Castilian is official nationwide; the other languages are official regionally

Spain in the EU: joined in 1986; 54 MEPs; voters approved the proposed EU constitution in a referendum in 2004

Spain in the world: At the crossroads of the Atlantic and the Mediterranean, Europe and Africa. During the 16th century, Spain was a powerful empire 'on which the sun did not set': it spread from South and Central America to East Asia. Spanish civil war (1936-39) was followed by international isolation under the dictator General Franco. King Carlos led Spain back to democracy after Franco's death in 1975. NATO member

PORTUGAL

Capital: Lisbon

Population: 10.5 million

Population growth rate: 0.39%

Average age: 38.2 years

Life expectancy at birth: 77.53 years (male 74.25 years, female 81.03 years)

Total land area: 92,391 sq km

Border countries: Spain

Coastline: 1,793 km

Religions: Roman Catholic 94%, Protestant and others 6%

Government type: parliamentary democracy, with unicameral Assembly of the Republic; the President is the chief of state

Administration: 18 districts and 2 autonomous regions

Economy: led by the service industry. Over the past decade, many firms run by the state have been privatised, and there have been many advances in the areas of finance and telecommunications

GDP: $194.8 billion, made up of agriculture 5.2%, industry 28.9%, services 65.9%

Industries: textiles, footwear, paper, rubber, plastic and metal products, chemicals, oil refining, fish canning, ceramics, electronics, transport and communications equipment, shipbuilding and refurbishment, wine, tourism

Labour force: 5.52 million

Unemployment: 7.3%

Currency: euro

Calling code: +351

Language: Portuguese

Portugal in the EU: joined 1986; 24 MEPs; the westernmost country in continental Europe

Portugal in the world: a founder member of NATO. A rich history of seafaring and discovery. An important colonial power, it lost a lot of its wealth and status after the devastating 1755 Lisbon earthquake and tsunami. In the 20th century, repressive governments ran Portugal, until a coup in 1974 ushered in democracy. This also led to independence for all Portugal's African colonies a year later

AUSTRIA

Capital: Vienna

Population: 8.1 million

Population growth rate: 0.11%

Average age: 40.44 years

Life expectancy at birth: 78.92 years (male 76.03 years, female 81.96 years)

Total land area: 83,870 sq km

Border countries: Czech Republic, Germany, Hungary, Italy, Liechtenstein, Slovakia, Slovenia, Switzerland

Coastline: 0 km (landlocked)

Religions: Roman Catholic 73.6%, Protestant 4.7%, Muslim 4.2%, other 3.5%, unspecified 2%, none 12%

Government type: federal republic; President is chief of state; bicameral Federal Assembly consists of Federal Council and the National Council; when the 'Freedom Party' joined a coalition in 2000, its extreme far-right views caused alarm in the EU and led to some sanctions against Austria

Administration: nine federal states

Economy: modern market economy, relying a lot on its service industry. 47% of the land area is forested, so timber is a key product. Attractive to foreign investors due to its strategic location at the crossroads of Central Europe, close to the new EU economies

GDP: $269.4 billion, made up of agriculture 2.3%, industry 30.8%, services 66.9%

Industries: construction, machinery, vehicles, food, metals, chemicals, lumber and wood processing, paper, communications equipment, tourism

Labour force: 3.49 million

Unemployment: 5.1%

Currency: euro

Calling code: +43

Languages: German (official nationwide), Slovene (official in Carinthia), Croatian and Hungarian (official in Burgenland)

Austria in the EU: joined in 1995; 18 MEPs

Austria in the world: Vienna is host to major international organisations, like the International Atomic Energy Agency; along with Switzerland, the only European country to declare itself 'permanently neutral'; under the Hapsburg dynasty, played a dominant role in Central Europe for centuries until 1918; has a rich cultural heritage and stunning mountain scenery

FINLAND

Capital: Helsinki

Population: 5.2 million

Population growth rate: 0.16%

Average age: 40.97 years

Life expectancy at birth: 78.35 years (male 74.82 years, female 82.02 years)

Total land area: 338,145 sq km

Border countries: Norway, Sweden, Russia

Coastline: 1,250 km (and has 187,888 lakes and 179,584 islands)

Religions: Lutheran National Church 84.2%, Greek Orthodox in Finland 1.1%, other Christian 1.1%, other 0.1%, none 13.5%

Government type: republic; President is chief of state and there is a unicameral parliament

Administration: 6 provinces

Economy: a modern industrial state with a high level of income per person. Manufacturing sector is strong, and Finland exports a lot of high-tech products like mobile phones (it is the home of Nokia). There is also an advanced social welfare system

GDP: $158.4 billion, made up of agriculture 3.1%, industry 30.4%, services 66.5%

Industries: metals, electronics, machinery and scientific instruments, shipbuilding, pulp and paper (two-thirds of Finland is covered in forest), foodstuffs, chemicals, textiles, clothing

Labour force: 2.61 million

Unemployment: 7.9%

Currency: euro

Calling code: +358

Languages: Finnish, Swedish

Finland in the EU: joined in 1995; 14 MEPs; the only Nordic EU state to adopt the euro

Finland in the world: lived for centuries under Swedish rule, then under the shadow of the powerful Soviet Union for much of 20th century, even after independence in 1917. Famous for its 'White Nights' in the far north: for ten weeks in the summer, the sun never sets (but also for eight weeks in winter the sun never rises)

SWEDEN

Capital: Stockholm

Population: 8.9 million

Population growth rate: 0.17%

Average age: 40.6 years

Life expectancy at birth: 80.4 years (male 78.19 years, female 82.74 years – one of the highest in the world)

Total land area: 449,964 sq km

Border countries: Finland and Norway

Coastline: 3,218 km

Religions: Lutheran 87%, Roman Catholic, Orthodox, Baptist, Muslim, Jewish, Buddhist

Government type: the Kingdom of Sweden is a constitutional monarchy; the monarch is the chief of state; there is a unicameral parliament

Administration: 21 counties

Economy: strong: a high standard of living based on mixing high-tech capitalism with big welfare benefits. Low unemployment

GDP: $266.5 billion, made up of agriculture 1.8%, industry 28.6%, services 69.7%

Industries: iron and steel, precision equipment (bearings, radio and telephone parts, armaments), wood pulp and paper products, processed foods, motor vehicles

Labour force: 4.49 million

Unemployment: 6%

Currency: krona

Calling code: +46

Languages: Swedish; small Sami- and Finnish-speaking minorities

Sweden in the EU: joined in 1995; 19 MEPs; Swedish voters said 'no' to adopting the euro in 2003

Sweden in the world: in the 17th and 18th centuries Sweden used warfare to expand its territory; it became a great power and grew to twice its present size. But the country went through the whole of the 20th century without any wars, taking a neutral stance. It is not a member of NATO. Many asylum seekers and refugees go to Sweden: over 10% of the population are immigrants

CYPRUS

Note: Cyprus has been divided between Greece and Turkey since 1974, when Turkish troops invaded the north. Cyprus is still divided after Greek Cypriots rejected a UN settlement in a referendum, while Turkish Cypriots approved it

Capital: Nicosia

Population: 807,000 (combined)

Population growth rate: 0.54%

Average age: 34.68 years

Life expectancy at birth: 77.65 years (male 75.29 years, female 80.13 years)

Total land area (Greek/Turkish areas combined): 9,250 sq km

Border countries: in the Middle East, south of Turkey, the third-largest island in the Mediterranean Sea (after Sicily and Sardinia)

Coastline: 648 km

Ethnic groups: Greek 77%, Turkish 18%, other 5%

Religions: Greek Orthodox 78%, Muslim 18%, Maronite, Armenian Apostolic, and other 4%

Government type: republic. Greek Cypriots control the only internationally recognised government: the President is the head of state; it has a unicameral House of Representatives

Economy: in the Republic of Cyprus, tourism and finance make up three-quarters of GDP. The Turkish Cypriot economy relies heavily on the Turkish government for support

GDP: Republic of Cyprus: $16.82 billion, made up of agriculture 3.8%, industry 20%, services 76.2%; North Cyprus: $4.54 billion, made up of agriculture 10.6%, industry 20.5%, services 68.9%

Labour force: Republic of Cyprus: 370,000, north Cyprus: 95,025

Unemployment: Republic of Cyprus: 3.5%; north Cyprus: 5.6%

Currency: Cyprus pound

Calling code: +357 or +90-392 in north

Languages: Greek, Turkish, English

Cyprus in the EU: joined in 2004; 6 MEPs; the island was still divided when Cyprus became a member of the EU. A member of the EU, so EU laws and benefits apply only to Greek Cypriots

Cyprus in the world: known as the birthplace of Aphrodite, mythical Greek goddess of love; defined by enmity between Greek and Turkish Cypriots; was once a colony of the UK (independence agreed in 1960)

CZECH REPUBLIC

Capital: Prague

Population: 10.2 million

Population growth rate: -0.05%

Average age: 38.97%

Life expectancy at birth: 76.02 years (male 72.74 years, female 79.49 years)

Total land area: 78,866 sq km

Border countries: Austria, Germany, Poland, Slovakia

Coastline: 0 km (landlocked)

Religions: Roman Catholic 26.8%, Protestant 2.1%, other 3.3%, unspecified 8.8%, unaffiliated 59% (2001 census)

Government type: parliamentary democracy; the President is the chief of state; a bicameral parliament consists of the Senate and the Chamber of Deputies

Administration: 13 regions

Economy: one of the most stable and prosperous of the post-Communist states of Central and Eastern Europe. Moves towards economic reform have been boosted by membership of the EU

GDP: $184.9 billion, made up of agriculture 3.4%, industry 39.3%, services 57.3%

Industries: metals, machinery and equipment, motor vehicles, glass, armaments

Labour force: 5.27 million

Unemployment: 9.1%

Currency: koruna

Calling code: +420

Language: Czech

The Czech Republic in the EU: joined in 2004; 24 MEPs

The Czech Republic in the world: Rich cultural history and architectural treasures. As the nation of Czechoslovakia, it gained freedom from decades of Soviet rule in the peaceful 'Velvet Revolution' in 1989, before a 'Velvet Divorce' into two nations, the Czech Republic and Slovakia, in 1993. Joined NATO in 1999

ESTONIA

Capital: Tallinn

Population: 1.3 million

Population growth rate: -0.65%

Average age: 39.06 years

Life expectancy at birth: 71.77 years (male 66.28 years, female 77.6 years)

Total land area: 45,226 sq km

Border countries: Latvia and Russia

Coastline: 3,794 km

Religions: Evangelical Lutheran 13.6%, Orthodox 12.8%, other Christian (including Methodist, Seventh-Day Adventist, Roman Catholic, Pentecostal) 1.4%, unaffiliated 34.1%, other and unspecified 32%, none 6.1% (2000 census)

Government type: parliamentary republic; the President is the chief of state; unicameral parliament; has experimented with internet voting

Administration: 15 counties

Economy: one of the strongest economies of the new member states, making a smooth transition to a modern market economy; has strong links with the West, and has pegged its currency to the euro. Estonia is doing especially well in electronics and telecommunications. Forest covers 47% of the land

GDP: $21.81 billion, made up of agriculture 4.1%, industry 29.1%, services 66.8%

Industries: engineering, electronics, wood and wood products, textiles, information technology, telecommunications

Labour force: 670,000

Unemployment: 9.2%

Currency: kroon

Calling code: +372

Languages: Estonian, Russian

Estonia in the EU: joined in 2004; 6 MEPs

Estonia in the world: gained independence in 1918, after centuries of Danish, Swedish, German and Russian rule. But the Soviet Union took control in 1940, and Estonia only got its freedom back in 1991, when communism collapsed. Joined NATO in 2004. The most northerly of the three former Soviet Baltic republics. The only country in the world where access to the internet is a 'human right'

HUNGARY

Capital: Budapest

Population: 9.8 million

Population growth rate: -0.26%

Average age: 38.57 years

Life expectancy at birth: 72.4 years
(male 68.18 years, female 76.89 years)

Total land area: 93,030 sq km

Border countries: Austria, Croatia, Romania, Serbia and Montenegro, Slovakia, Slovenia, Ukraine

Coastline: 0 km (landlocked)

Religions: Roman Catholic 51.9%, Calvinist 15.9%, Lutheran 3%, Greek Catholic 2.6%, other Christian 1%, other or unspecified 11.1%, unaffiliated 14.5%

Government type: parliamentary democracy; the President is chief of state and there is a unicameral National Assembly

Administration: 19 counties, 20 urban counties, and 1 capital city

Economy: moved from a centrally planned to a market economy; a lot of foreign businesses own and invest in Hungarian firms. The private sector accounts for more than 80% of GDP

GDP: $159 billion, made up of agriculture 3.9%, industry 30.9%, services 65.3%

Industries: mining, metals, construction materials, processed foods, textiles, chemicals, pharmaceuticals, motor vehicles

Labour force: 4.18 million

Unemployment: 7.1%

Currency: forint

Calling code: +36

Language: Hungarian

Hungary in the EU: joined in 2004; 24 MEPs

Hungary in the world: member of NATO since 1999; strategically located on main land routes between Western Europe and Balkan Peninsula, and between Ukraine and Mediterranean basin; has largest lake in Europe, Lake Balaton; was under Communist rule after World War II until the collapse of the Soviet Union: Hungary helped speed things up by opening its border with Austria so East Germans could escape to the west; a colourful mix of peoples: along with the majority Magyars, there are Roma, German, Slovak, Croat, Serb and Romanian minorities; amongst other things, Hungarians invented the match, the theory of the hydrogen bomb and the ballpoint pen

LATVIA

Capital: Riga

Population: 2.3 million

Population growth rate: -0.69%

Average age: 39.12 years

Life expectancy at birth: 71.05 years

Total land area: 64,589 sq km

Border countries: Belarus, Estonia, Lithuania, Russia

Coastline: 531 km

Ethnic groups: Latvian 57.7%, Russian 29.6%, Belarusian 4.1%, Ukrainian 2.7%, Polish 2.5%, Lithuanian 1.4%, other 2%

Religions: Lutheran, Roman Catholic, Russian Orthodox

Government type: parliamentary democracy; the President is the chief of state, the Prime Minister is the head of the government and there is a unicameral parliament

Administration: 26 counties and 7 municipalities

Economy: the Latvian economy was badly hit by the 1998 Russian financial crisis. But since then it has changed its focus to deal with other EU countries, and growth rates have been high. Most companies, banks and real estate have been privatised, but some large enterprises are still in the hands of the state

GDP: $29.42 billion, made up of agriculture 4.1%, industry 26%, services 69.9%

Industries: vehicles, synthetics, farm machinery, fertilisers, washing machines, radios, electronics, pharmaceuticals, processed foods, textiles

Labour force: 1.11 million

Unemployment: 8.8%

Currency: lat

Calling code: +371

Languages: Latvian (official) 58.2%, Russian 37.5%, Lithuanian and other 4.3% (2000 census)

Latvia in the EU: joined 2004; 9 MEPs

Latvia in the world: under foreign control from the 13th to the 20th centuries; brief spell of independence before Soviet rule in the 1940s, which finally ended in 1991; the middle of the three former Soviet Baltic republics; tensions with Russia over border issues; member of World Trade Organization, and joined NATO in 2004 shortly before membership of the EU – all impossible to imagine during the Soviet days

LITHUANIA

Capital: Vilnius

Population: 3.4 million

Population growth rate: -0.3%

Average age: 37.83 years

Life expectancy at birth: 73.97 years (male 68.94 years, female 79.28 years)

Total land area: 65,200 sq km

Border countries: Belarus, Latvia, Poland, Russia

Coastline: 99 km

Religions: Roman Catholic 79%, Russian Orthodox 4.1%, Protestant (including Lutheran and Evangelical Christian Baptist) 1.9%, other or unspecified 5.5%, none 9.5% (2001 census)

Government type: parliamentary democracy, unicameral parliament, President is head of state

Administration: 10 counties

Economy: Lithuania used to trade more with Russia than either of its Baltic state neighbours, but after the Russian financial crisis in 1998 it was forced to turn more to the West. It was given membership of the World Trade Organisation in 2001, and growth rates in recent years have been high, although a lot of people in the country are still poor

GDP: $49.38 billion, made up of agriculture 5.7%, industry 32.4%, services 62%

Industries: metal-cutting machine tools, electric motors, television sets, refrigerators and freezers, petroleum refining, shipbuilding (small ships), furniture making, textiles, food processing, fertilisers, agricultural machinery, optical equipment, electronic components, computers, amber

Labour force: 1.61 million

Unemployment: 5.3%

Currency: lita

Calling code: +370

Languages: Lithuanian (official) 82%, Russian 8%, Polish 5.6%, other and unspecified 4.4% also spoken (2001 census)

Lithuania in the EU: joined 2004; 13 MEPs

Lithuania in the world: Lithuania helped to hasten the end of Soviet rule with its 'Singing Revolution'; it became the first of the Soviet republics to declare its independence in 1990, after 50 years of rule by Moscow. The last Russian troops withdrew in 1993. Lithuania joined NATO in spring 2004

MALTA

Capital: Valletta

Population: 397,000

Population growth rate: 0.42%

Average age: 38.36 years

Life expectancy at birth: 78.86 years (male 76.7 years, female 81.15 years)

Total land area: 316 sq km

Border countries: none; Malta comprises an archipelago: only the three largest islands are inhabited

Coastline: 196.8 km

Religions: Roman Catholic 98%

Government type: republic; unicameral House of Representatives; President is chief of state

Administration: governed directly from Valletta

Economy: Malta's main source of income is tourism: because of tourist arrivals, the population triples every year. It has an attractive geographic location and a hard-working labour force. The economy also depends on foreign trade and manufacturing

GDP: $7.485 billion, made up of agriculture 3%, industry 23%, services 74%

Industries: tourism, electronics, shipbuilding and repair, construction, food and beverages, textiles, footwear, clothing, tobacco

Labour force: 160,000

Unemployment: 7%

Currency: Maltese lira

Calling code: +356

Languages: Maltese, English

Malta in the EU: joined 2004, the smallest of the ten new countries welcomed into the club; 5 MEPs

Malta in the world: a history of colonial rule going back centuries: Phoenicians, Greeks, Romans, Arabs, the French and the British have all colonised Malta

POLAND

Capital: Warsaw
Population: 38.5 million
Population growth rate: 0.03%
Average age: 36.43 years
Life expectancy at birth: 74.74 years (male 70.71 years, female 79.03 years)
Total land area: 312,685 sq km
Border countries: Belarus, Czech Republic, Germany, Lithuania, Russia, Slovakia, Ukraine
Coastline: 491 km
Religions: Roman Catholic 89.8% (about 75% practising), Eastern Orthodox 1.3%, Protestant 0.3%, other 0.3%, unspecified 8.3% (2002)
Government type: democratic republic; Council of Ministers led by Prime Minister; parliament with upper and lower house; President is head of state, chosen by popular vote
Administration: 16 provinces
Economy: Poland has made significant market reforms: many state-owned companies are now run by private businesses. Unemployment is the highest in the EU, with widespread poverty in rural areas. Agriculture is very important: 16% of the population work in farming. Many farms are small and inefficient, but Poland is benefiting from billions of euros in EU funds, and farmers have begun to gain through higher food prices and subsidies
GDP: $489.3 billion, made up of agriculture 2.8%, industry 31.7%, services 65.5%
Industries: machine building, iron and steel, coal mining, chemicals, shipbuilding, food processing, glass, beverages, textiles
Labour force: 17.1 million: 16% are farmers
Unemployment: 18.3%
Currency: zloty
Calling code: +48
Language: Polish
Poland in the EU: joined 2004; 54 MEPs; a key location at one of the EU's external borders
Poland in the world: at the centre of Europe; has a thousand-year history: sometimes independent, sometimes dominated by others; several million people, half of them Jews, died in World War II. Poland was a key player in the first moves away from communist rule in the 1980s; joined NATO in 1999; raised its profile internationally when it sent Polish troops to support the US-led invasion of Iraq

SLOVAKIA

Capital: Bratislava
Population: 5.4 million
Population growth rate: 0.15%
Average age: 35.43 years (male 33.85 years, female 37.25 years)
Life expectancy at birth: 74.5 years (male 70.76 years, female 78.89 years)
Total land area: 49,033 sq km
Border countries: Austria, Czech Republic, Hungary, Poland, Ukraine
Coastline: 0 km (landlocked)
Religions: Roman Catholic 68.9%, Protestant 10.8%, Greek Catholic 4.1%, other or unspecified 3.2%, none 13% (2001 census)
Government type: parliamentary democracy with a unicameral National Council of the Slovak Republic
Administration: 8 regions
Economy: Slovakia is a popular place for foreign investors: for example, most banks are now in foreign hands. Many reforms have been made and economic growth has been strong, though unemployment is still a worry
GDP: $85.14, billion made up of agriculture 3.6%, industry 29.7%, services 66.7%
Industries: metals, food and beverages, electricity, gas, coke, oil, nuclear fuel, chemicals and manmade fibres, machinery, paper and printing, earthenware and ceramics, transport vehicles, textiles, electrical and optical apparatus, rubber products
Labour force: 2.62 million
Unemployment: 11.5%
Currency: koruna
Calling code: +421
Languages: Slovak; about 10% of population speak Hungarian
Slovakia in the EU: joined in 2004
Slovakia in the world: at the heart of Europe, with a history closely linked to its neighbours, but proud of its own distinct language and culture; was part of Czechoslovakia until the 'Velvet Divorce' in 1993, when the two countries agreed to split up; member of NATO since 2004

SLOVENIA

Capital: Ljubljana

Population: 2 million

Population growth rate: -0.03%

Average age: 40.23 years (male 38.65 years, female 41.75 years)

Life expectancy at birth: 76.14 years

Total land area: 20,273 sq km

Border countries: Austria, Croatia, Hungary, Italy

Coastline: 46.6 km

Religions: Catholic 57.8%, Orthodox 2.3%, other Christian 0.9%, Muslim 2.4%, unaffiliated 3.5%, other or unspecified 23%, none 10.1% (2002 census)

Government type: parliamentary democratic republic: a bicameral parliament consisting of a National Assembly and National Council

Administration: 182 municipalities and 11 urban municipalities

Economy: Slovenia was always one of the most prosperous regions of the former Yugoslavia, and people have a better income per head than in any of the other EU countries that joined in 2004. The move from socialist economy to capitalist free market has been smooth. Foreign investment is healthy and unemployment has gone down.

GDP: $42.09 billion, made up of agriculture 2.8%, industry 36.9%, services 60.3%

Industries: iron, steel and aluminium products, lead and zinc smelting, electronics (including military electronics), trucks, electric power equipment, wood products, textiles, chemicals, machine tools

Labour force: 920,000

Unemployment: 9.8%

Currency: tolar

Calling code: +386

Official language: Slovene

Slovenia in the EU: joined in 2004; the only former Yugoslav republic to be in the first wave of candidates for membership

Slovenia in the world: spectacular mountains and thick forests; gained independence from Yugoslavia after a 10-day war in 1991; member of NATO

SOME EU ACHIEVEMENTS

- There is now a single market that makes it easier for EU nations to buy and sell to each other. Since 2002, people in 12 countries have been using a single currency, called the euro.
- The EU has one of the most powerful economies in the world, and gives more money than anyone else to help developing countries.
- All EU countries (except Britain and Ireland) have agreed to scrap internal border controls, so people can travel across most of the region without passport checks.
- Through EU programmes like 'Erasmus', some two million young people have studied in another European country.
- The Union helps its poorer regions by giving money for things like transport projects, and training people to give them new skills.
- Because of laws on the environment, Europe's rivers and beaches have become cleaner and there is less pollution from vehicles.
- EU citizens are free to live, work, vote and retire in the country of their choice.

Waiting in the wings

Eight more countries are hoping to join the European Union.

BULGARIA

Hoping for membership by 2007 or 2008
Capital: Sofia
Population: 7.8 million
Total land area: 110,994 sq km
Official language: Bulgarian
Currency: lev
Member of NATO since 2004

ROMANIA

Hoping for membership by 2007 or 2008
Capital: Bucharest
Population: 22.2 million
Total land area: 238,391 sq km
Official language: Romanian
Currency: new leu
Member of NATO since 2004

CROATIA

Began talks in 2005 on accession to the EU: could join by 2010

Capital: Zagreb
Population: 4.4 million
Total land area: 56,594 sq km
Official language: Croatian
Currency: kuna

TURKEY

Began talks in 2005 on accession to the EU: could join by 2015; the continents of Europe and Asia meet in Turkey
Capital: Ankara
Population: 73.3 million
Total land area: 779,452 sq km
Official language: Turkish
Currency: New Turkish lira

ALBANIA

BOSNIA-HERCEGOVINA

MACEDONIA

SERBIA MONTENEGRO

Montenegro voted for independence from Serbia in May 2006.

The EU says these Balkan countries can become members one day.
They need to meet certain standards on:
- democracy
- rule of law
- having a market economy
- sticking to EU goals on political and economic union.

THE EUROPEAN UNION

Location: Europe, between Belarus, Ukraine, Russia, southeastern Europe and the North Atlantic Ocean

Capital: Brussels, Belgium. The Council of the EU meets in Brussels, the Parliament in Strasbourg, France, and the Court of Justice in Luxembourg

Population: 456,953,258

Population growth rate: 0.15%

Fertility rate: 1.47 children born for every woman in the EU

Age distribution: 0-14 years: 16.03%, 15-64 years: 67.17%, 65 years and over: 16.81%

Life expectancy at birth: 81.6 years (male 78.3 years, female 75.1 years)

Net migration: 1.5 migrants per 1,000

Total land area: 3,976,372 sq km

Border countries: Albania, Andorra, Belarus, Bulgaria, Croatia, Holy See, Liechtenstein, Macedonia, Monaco, Norway, Romania, Russia, San Marino, Serbia and Montenegro, Switzerland, Turkey, Ukraine (data for European Continent only)

Lowest/highest point: Lammefjord, Denmark -7 m; Zuidplaspolder, Netherlands -7 m/ Mont Blanc, France 4,807 m

Coastline: 65,413.9 km

Natural hazards: from flooding in coastal areas, to avalanches in mountains; from volcanoes in Italy to earthquakes in the south; from droughts in southern Europe to ice floes in the Baltic

Religions: Roman Catholic, Protestant, Orthodox, Muslim, Jewish

Government type: a hybrid intergovernmental organisation.

European Commission: member governments decide who will be the President of the Commission; the President-designate chooses the other members; the European Parliament confirms the whole Commission for a five-year term

European Council: the main decision-making body: it brings together heads of state and government and the President of the Commission at least twice a year to push for progress on major EU issues

European Parliament: 732 seats split among member states according to their population. EU voters (18 and over) choose members of parliament for five-year term

Economy: the EU tries to reach agreement between 25 nations on all economic issues, but member states do not always agree. There is a big

range of average yearly income. Twelve EU member states adopted the euro as their common currency on 1 January 1999. The UK, Sweden and Denmark did not. The EU's ten new countries (since 2004) may adopt the euro if they meet a series of tests

GDP: $12.18 trillion (highest in the world), made up of agriculture 2.2%, industry 27.3%, services 70.5%

Industries: among the world's largest and most technologically advanced, the European Union industrial base includes: metal production and processing, metal products, petroleum, coal, cement, chemicals, pharmaceuticals, aerospace, rail transportation equipment, passenger and commercial vehicles, construction equipment, industrial equipment, shipbuilding, electrical power equipment, machine tools and automated manufacturing systems, electronics and telecommunications equipment, fishing, food and beverage processing, furniture, paper, textiles, tourism

Labour force: 218.5 million made up of agriculture 4.5%, industry 27.4%, services 66.9%

Unemployment: 9.4%

Exports: $1.318 trillion (these do not include trade between EU countries); export partners US 24.2%, Switzerland 7.7%, China 5%, Russia 4.7%

Imports: $1,402 trillion (not including EU countries' trade with each other) made up of US 15.3%, China 12.4%, Russia 7.8%, Japan 7.2%

Currencies: euro, British pound, Danish kroner, Swedish kroner, Cypriot pound, koruny (Czech Republic), krooni (Estonia), forint (Hungary), lati (Latvia), litai (Lithuania), Maltese liri, zloty (Poland), koruny (Slovakia), tolar (Slovenia)

Official languages: Czech, Danish, Dutch, English, Estonian, Finnish, French, German, Greek, Hungarian, Italian, Latvian, Lithuanian, Maltese, Polish, Portuguese, Slovak, Slovene, Spanish, Swedish; Irish (Gaelic) will become the 21st language in 2007

EU in the world: has its own flag, anthem, founding date and currency. Issues of common foreign and security policies are work in progress

Glossary and websites

Accession   Signing up to become a member.

Asylum   The chance for people to live safely in a new country, if it is dangerous for them to live in their own.

Audit   A close examination of how an organisation is run, and whether it is sticking to the rules.

Co-decision   Making a decision by reaching agreement with each other.

Development aid   Money that is given to people who need help, especially in poorer countries.

Democracy   A system where the people can choose who runs their country.

Discrimination   Unfair treatment.

Diversity   Variety.

Economy   The money and resources of a country, and how the government looks after them.

EU Constitution   A set of guidelines and rules on the way the EU should be run.

EU Enlargement   Making the EU club bigger by allowing new members to join.

EU Treaty   Agreements made between member states of the EU.

Federation   A system of government where states are united but decide some things for themselves.

Free trade   Buying and selling without rules giving an unfair advantage to one side or the other.

GDP or Gross Domestic Product   The value of everything that a country produces in one year.

Immigration   Coming into a foreign country to live there.

Institution   An organisation with its own rules and customs.

Monetary policy   Agreements on how to handle money matters.

Referendum   The chance for people to vote on an important issue.

Parliament   A place where politicians meet to decide the laws of the country.

Peacekeeping missions   Troops sent to a country to maintain peace after conflict.

Prosperity   Wealth.

Reunified   Countries joining together again after they have been split up.

Single market   A trading area with no barriers to the free movement of money, people and goods.

Subsidies   Money given to try to fix prices at a certain level.

Taxation   Rules on how much money people and businesses must pay to the state, depending on how much they earn.

The United Nations   An international organisation that tries to push for peace between different countries.

http://europa.eu.int/
Gateway to the official European Union website

http://europa.eu.int/europago/welcome.jsp
'Europe is fun' – EU website for younger readers

www.europarl.eu.int/news/public/default_en.htm
Official European Parliament website

www.europa.eu.int/comm/index_en.htm
Official EU Commission website

www.europa.eu.int/comm/index_en.htm
Official EU Council website

http://www.eurunion.org/infores/teaching/Young/fun.htm
EU guide for young people, with links to further reading materials and websites for individual countries

www.bbc.co.uk/eu
'Inside Europe: a guide to the changing face of the European Union': on the BBC news website, an excellent resource for older readers

http://news.bbc.co.uk/cbbcnews/hi/guides/default.stm
BBC Newsround guide to the EU – choose it from drop-down list

http://www.cia.gov/cia/publications/factbook/
CIA World Factbook: guides available to each EU country, and the EU itself

http://www.wikipedia.org
Gateway to free online encyclopaedia with more facts about EU countries

www.guardian.co.uk/eu
Useful EU resource for older readers

Index